GRANOLA MADNESS

Granola Madness

The Ultimate Granola Cookbook

by
Donna Wallstin and Katherine Dieter

New World Library
Novato, California

New World Library
14 Pamaron Way
Novato, California 94949

Cover design: Kathy Warriner
Illustrations: Jenna Jones
Text design: Aaron Kenedi

Library of Congress Cataloging-in-Publication Data
Wallstin, Donna.
Granola Madness : the ultimate granola cookbook / by Donna Wallstin and Katherine Dieter
p. cm.
ISBN 1-880032-89-9 (pbk. : alk. paper)
1. Cookery (Granola) I. Dieter, Katherine. II Title.
TX809.G7W35 1996 96-18943
641.6'31--dc20 CIP

First printing, September 1996
Printed in the U.S.A on acid-free paper
Distributed to the trade by Publishers Group West

10 9 8 7 6 5 4 3 2 1

CONTENTS

Basic granola recipes with varying characteristics (chewy, crunchy) and suggestions for variations on the basics. These recipes are distinguished by technique, texture, adaptability, and nutritional content.

Basic Recipes:

Part II ONE SCREW LOOSE

This is where the "madness" begins — with endless combinations of ingredients.

Recipes:

Part III COMPLETELY NUTS 39

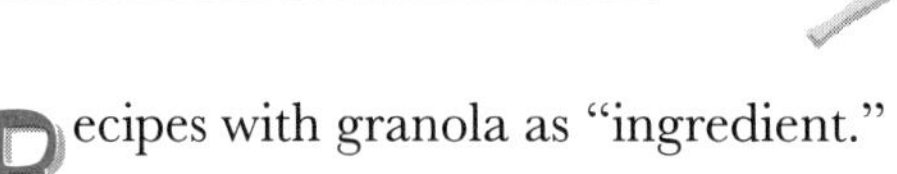

Recipes with granola as "ingredient."

Breads

Cobblers, Desserts, and Toppings

Where did it Come From?

In the mid-1800s, a Presbyterian minister from Philadelphia named Sylvester Graham was at the forefront of a vegetarian "craze" that swept across the country. At the time, most Americans were eating salt beef and pork, hominy, condiments, and white bread. The reverend denounced the consumption of these things on moral and medical grounds and preached the virtues of, among other things, whole grain flour, which soon became known as "Graham" flour.

Influenced by Graham, a Dr. Jackson from New York made a heavy dough out of Graham flour and water, baked it slowly until the loaves were very dry, broke the loaves up into small chunks and baked them again, finally grinding the brittle chunks into even smaller pieces and calling this first modern breakfast cereal "Granula."

When a sanitarium in Battle Creek, Michigan, run by Graham's followers failed in 1866, the Seventh Day Adventist Church took it over. (The leader of this church, Ellen White, had recently had a revelation on the subject of human diet, and a "pure" diet — meatless, stimulantless — became official Church policy.) Eventually the Church brought in the son of a prominent Adventist family to help legitimize the medical benefits of the vegetarian diet. His name was Dr. John Harvey Kellogg.

Continually experimenting with nuts, legumes, and grains, Dr. Kellogg soon came up with a breakfast food made of wheat, oats, and corn meal baked into biscuits and then ground up. He named this concoction "Granula" and was promptly sued by Dr. Jackson of New York. (Such an American story.)

Forced to change the name, Kellogg settled for "Granola," which remained a trademark for many years (even though Dr. Kellogg soon lost interest in cereals and turned his attention to yogurt and nut butters, eventually publishing a paper interestingly titled, "Nuts May Save the Race").

"Granola" has since become associated with an attitude — a lifestyle — that espouses purity, simplicity, and good health. It enjoyed a radical resurgence in the 1960s and remains a staple in many American homes. Unfortunately, the cost of granola has risen dramatically while the quality lags behind. Even the best granola available can't compare to the satisfying golden crunch of homemade.

We have learned far more about nutrition since the conception of granola, and while there are ingredients in these recipes that boost nutrition, we certainly do not suggest you limit your diet to granola alone. A healthy diet is a varied diet. You will find no "Granola Meatloaf" or "Granola Vegetable Spaghetti," in this eclectic collection, only reasonable leaps of culinary imagination.

As the authors of *Granola Madness*, we make no claim to an ability to save the human race, but we do hope to make life, especially mornings, more bearable — maybe even enjoyable.

The Nature of Homemade Granola

"Bake to a golden crispness" is instructed in most of the granola recipes in this book. Achieving this result begins with baking's basic sequence: to combine wet and dry ingredients, then bake.

Rolled grains are the foundation of the dry ingredients, combined with a liquid sweetener or flavoring, and maybe some oil for texture. The essence of granola — simple with subtle complexities — is the essence of most good things. What we've added to this formula is our brand of madness — easy, customized, homemade granola, that will be the best you will ever eat.

CLUMP AND CRUMBLE

The "clump-to-crumble ratio" is for many an important granola characteristic. The "clump" provides a crunchy mouthful of every taste and texture offered in the recipe, supported by the unique character of each ingredient of the granola that makes up the "crumble." Clump is determined by the proportion of liquid to dry ingredients, and the particular characteristics of the liquid ingredients.

HONEY, thick and sticky, contributes most to give granola a clumpy consistency. Brown rice syrup — with the same consistency as honey — gives granola a light, crisp texture with a nice clump-to-crumble ratio, and a less-sweet flavor.

CRISPNESS

Crisp texture is an ideal trait. It can be achieved in a number of ways, depending on which recipe and techniques you use.

ADDING OIL to a batch of granola, particularly if you are not adding nuts or seeds, will give the grains a crisp texture after the granola is baked and cooled. Adding oil or melted butter also imparts a richer flavor. Adding oil, however, is always optional, particularly if minimizing fat is your goal.

A FEW WORDS ON INGREDIENTS

Buy the best ingredients you can get your hands on, as few or as many as you like. This is where you should be fanatical, uncompromising, and just plain picky.

A FEW TECHNIQUES

TOASTING THE GRAINS:

Toasting the grains before combining with the other ingredients will assure a crisper granola, and enhance the grains' nutty flavors. The toasting process can be done in the oven or on the stove.

In the oven: Place the grains in an even layer (no more than 1-inch deep) in a roasting pan. Toast in a preheated 325°F oven for 5-7 minutes, stirring every few minutes to heat evenly. Each grain should be warmed through and crisp to the bite. A slight deepening of color may occur but that is not the characteristic to look for during this step. Over-toasting will scorch the grains and give them a bitter flavor.

On the stove: Toast the grains in a large heavy-bottomed skillet (in a 1-inch deep layer; do this in batches if necessary) over medium heat. Stir frequently, until grains are fragrant and evenly heated through — about 8 minutes.

TO TOAST OR NOT TO TOAST

Grains have a more chewy texture when they are not toasted. We strongly suggest toasting the grains when making the "raw" granola recipes. The result, particularly the taste, is much better.

WARMING THE LIQUIDS

This accomplishes a few things:

1) assures that all the characteristics of the liquid ingredients — their flavors and textures — are thoroughly combined;

2) helps thick, sticky honey, molasses, maple syrup, etc., flow more easily so that they mix evenly with all the ingredients;

3) the liquid ingredients are key flavor agents; they are enhanced when warmed. Add spices and citrus zest to the warm liquids to enhance the flavors of these ingredients before mixing them into a batch of granola.

COMBINING THE "DRY" WITH THE "LIQUID"

When you have combined all the ingredients for your recipe, stir them together thoroughly, distributing them evenly. Be sure that the grains and other dry ingredients have absorbed, or are completely coated with, the liquid ingredients. This assures uniformity in flavor and texture.

WHILE BAKING

Bake in thin, even layers. Spread the granola in level 1-inch layers so that it bakes quickly and evenly with minimal amounts of stirring. Divide a large batch of granola between 2 large pans.

Stir and respread the granola in the pan every 5 minutes or so. This is important because the granola cooks more quickly at the edges of the pan. Those "edges" need to be redistributed at intervals so that everything bakes evenly. The flavor from burnt nuts or grains will taint the flavor of the whole batch.

Don't bake the dried fruits with the granola — they will dry out and become bitter tasting. Leave them to be mixed in directly after the granola comes out of the oven and before it cools — they will stick to the warm mass and their sweet chewiness will become integral to the clumpy texture of the finished granola.

PROOFING THE YEAST

This step assures that the yeast is active. The yeast is stirred into warm water (about 100°F) often with a bit of sugar (honey, molasses, as the case may be). It then expands, becoming "creamy," and ferments, becoming bubbly. The yeast is then ready for the next stage of the recipe.

TO PUREE (pumpkin, butternut, acorn, or any winter squash, and sweet potato)

Roast these vegetables to retain their nutrients and best flavor before pureeing. This dry method of cooking also assures that the texture of the puree won't be too soggy.

Preheat oven to 375°F.

For Pumpkins and Winter Squash: Split the squash and scoop out the seeds. Rub the cut surface and the skin with a bit of cooking oil, and season the flesh with a pinch or two of salt. Place the vegetable cut side down on a baking sheet lined with parchment paper or tin foil. Roast until a sharp knife point pierces easily. When cool, scoop the flesh away from the skin with a spoon. Force through a mesh sieve or food mill, or puree in a food processor.

For Sweet Potatoes: Pierce the potatoes a few times with a fork. Roast them whole until they are soft and give easily when squeezed gently. Cool, then peel. Force the potato through a food mill or a mesh sieve, or mash with a potato masher.

SANITY
The Basic Recipes

Simple Granola

5 1/2 cups "thick cut" rolled oats
1/2 cup honey or maple syrup, or a combined 1/4 cup of each
1/3 cup canola oil

Preheat oven to 325°F.

Combine the honey (and/or maple syrup), oil, and salt in a sauce pan; heat until just warm. In a large bowl, add the warmed liquid ingredients to the oats and stir until well combined. Spread the mixture evenly in a shallow roasting pan. Bake for about 20 minutes, stirring and respreading every 5 minutes until light golden brown. Cool completely before storing in an airtight container.

This recipe involves only what is essential to create the characteristic texture (the crunch and crumble) and sweetness of this stuff called "granola."

Honey makes for a sweeter result, while maple syrup adds a subtle, smooth sweetness; combined, they give the best flavor and texture.

Granola
(makes 8 cups)

A word about rolled oats:

Use the "thick cut" rolled oats. These are whole, chewy ovals of oat grains with a moist, dense texture and sweet nutty flavor. Avoid the commercial brands of "regular" or "quick-cooking" oatmeals.

1/2 cup chopped walnuts
2 tablespoons whole wheat pastry flour
1/2 cup barley malt (or other sweetener)
1/2 teaspoon cinnamon
1/2 cup raisins
1 cup sunflower seeds
4 cups rolled oats

Preheat oven to 325°F.

Combine walnuts, sunflower seeds, flour, oats; spread on a sheet pan and toast in the oven for 5 minutes.

Combine barley malt, cinnamon, and vanilla in a sauce pan; heat until warm.

In a large bowl, thoroughly combine the dry toasted ingredients with the liquid ingredients. Spread in a lightly oiled roasting pan and roast, stirring and respreading every 5 minutes, until light golden brown — about 20 minutes. Remove to a bowl and stir in raisins. Cool completely. Store in an airtight container.

Another Granola
(makes 9 cups)

6 cups rolled oats
1 cup sunflower seeds
1/2 cup chopped walnuts
3 tablespoons honey
1/3 cup barley malt
1/2 cup canola oil
1/4 cup water (or fruit juice), hot
1 cup raisins

The "other" granola. With a hint of malt, this granola is less sweet. An ideal base for trail mix, it stands up to some salty additions. Try a variety of nuts (peanuts), dried fruit, and seeds (pumpkin) or embellish the granola with some of the suggested options in the sidebar.

Preheat oven to 325°F.

In a large bowl combine rolled oats, sunflower seeds, walnuts. In a saucepan combine honey, barley malt, oil, and water (or fruit juice). Heat until hot, not boiling. Add to oats mixture and mix thoroughly. Spread in thin, even layers in roasting pans. Bake, stirring occasionally, for 15-20 minutes — until golden brown. Remove from oven and stir in raisins. Cool in pan on cooling rack.

Options:

Add desired amount at whim:
— crushed fennel seeds, the zest of one orange (add both just before baking), and dried cranberries.
— dried bananas and carob or semi-sweet chocolate chips (add chips only after granola is completely cooled).
— dried cherries, almonds, and chocolate chips.

WRITERS' GRANOLA

Where it all began.... Donna was a private chef at a writers' retreat when she started making granola as a breakfast staple. When she couldn't keep up with the demand, she knew she had something extraordinary. This recipe has become her favorite — easy, just a few ingredients, clumpy texture, and no added oil.

4 cups rolled oats
2/3 cup whole raw almonds
2/3 cup pecan halves
1/4 cup sesame seeds
1/4 cup honey
1/4 cup maple syrup
1 1/2 cups raisins

Preheat the oven to 325°F.

Toast the oats (see page 13), then combine with nuts and sesame seeds in a large bowl. In a saucepan, gently warm the honey and maple syrup; then add to oats mixture and stir until thoroughly combined. Spread in a thin, even layer in a roasting pan. Bake, stirring and respreading every 5 minutes, until golden brown — 20-25 minutes.

Remove from oven and stir in raisins. Press into an even layer and allow to cool in a solid mass. Break into pieces and store in airtight container. Serve crumbled to desired clumpiness.

RAW GRANOLA
(serve hot or cold)

Note:

Be careful when grinding the nuts in a food processor, you can very easily end up with nut butter. Use the pulsing button and keep a close watch. The nuts should begin to give off their oils. Alternatively, use a nut grinder.

3 cups rolled oats
3 cups rolled barley, wheat, or rye (or combination of these)
1 cup toasted wheat germ
1 cup sunflower seeds
1/4 cup sesame seeds
1 1/2 cups almonds
1 cup nuts (walnuts, pecans, hazelnuts — whatever you like)
1 cup raisins
1 cup chopped dried fruit (apples, apricots, dates, pears, etc.)
1 teaspoon (or to taste) cinnamon
Fresh grated nutmeg to taste

Combine the grains and the spices. Toast as described on page 13. Toast the nuts in a 325°F oven until lightly golden. Grind a cup of the nuts in a food processor to the consistency of course meal (see note). Combine all ingredients thoroughly.

SERVE COLD, sweetened with honey, molasses, maple syrup, brown sugar, or any perfectly ripe fresh fruit, and your choice of milk. SERVE HOT, simply by adding hot milk, or for a more porridge-like consistency, cook 1 cup granola with 1 1/2 cups water or milk and a dash of salt over medium heat for 5 minutes. Then add your favorite hot cereal embellishments.

ONE SCREW LOOSE

The Madness Begins....

Queen Granola

4 cups rolled oats
$^{2}/_{3}$ cup whole wheat pastry flour
$^{1}/_{2}$ cup sunflower seeds
$^{1}/_{2}$ cup chopped walnuts
$^{2}/_{3}$ cup maple syrup
$^{2}/_{3}$ cup canola oil
2 tablespoons vanilla
1 teaspoon cinnamon
$^{1}/_{4}$ teaspoon salt
2 cups raisins

Preheat oven to 325°F.

Combine oil, maple syrup, vanilla, cinnamon, and salt in a sauce pan; heat until warm. In a large bowl combine remaining ingredients (except raisins). Then add the warmed liquid ingredients and combine thoroughly. Spread on a sheet pan or in a roasting pan; bake, turning and respreading every 5 minutes, until golden brown — 20-25 minutes. Remove to a bowl and stir in raisins. Cool completely.

Green Granola

*

Or any commercial spirulina protein powder available in most health food stores.

4 cups rolled oats (other rolled grains or combinations of them)
2/3 cup Super Green Spirulina Protein Powder*
4 tablespoons sesame seeds
1/3 cup sunflower seeds
2 tablespoons molasses
1/3 cup honey
1/4 cup canola oil

Preheat oven to 325°F.

Toast the oats (see page 13). Thoroughly combine the toasted oats, protein powder, sesame and sunflower seeds. In a small saucepan, warm the molasses, honey and canola oil; stir to blend. Add to the oats mixture and stir until well combined and all the dry ingredients are coated with the honey mixture. Spread in a thin, even layer in a roasting pan. Bake, stirring and respreading into an even layer every 5 minutes, until granola is lightly browned — about 20 minutes.

Maple Pecan Granola

8 cups rolled oats
1 cup course chopped pecans
1 teaspoon cinnamon
1/2 teaspoon nutmeg
1/3 cup maple syrup
1/3 cup orange juice
1/4 cup canola oil
2 teaspoons grated orange zest (or finely minced)
1 cup raisins (or chopped dates or apricots)

Preheat oven to 350°F.

Combine first 4 ingredients in a large bowl. In a saucepan heat together oil, orange juice, maple syrup, and orange zest until hot (do not boil). Pour over the oat mixture and combine thoroughly. Divide between 2 roasting pans; bake for 1/2 hour stirring every 10 minutes. Remove to a bowl and stir in dried fruit. Cool completely.

Orange Pecan Granola

4 cups rolled oats
3/4 cup pecan pieces
1/3 cup sunflower seeds
2 tablespoons molasses
1/3 cup honey
1/4 cup fresh orange juice

Toast the oats (see page 13), then combine with the pecans and sunflower seeds. In a saucepan, warm the molasses, honey, and orange juice, stirring to combine. Add to the oats mixture and stir thoroughly to coat completely. Spread in a roasting pan. Bake, stirring and respreading occasionally, until golden brown and crisp — about 20 minutes.

Molasses

To produce molasses, the juice from crushed sugarcane is boiled in vacuum vats. The sugar crystallizes and is separated from the molasses. The separation process is repeated and with each boiling — or "strike" — the result is a stronger, darker, and less sweet syrup. Table-grade molasses from the first strike is variously labeled "light," "mild," or "Barbados" style (the style recommended for these recipes).

Honey Almond Granola

6 cups rolled oats
1/2 cup sunflower seeds
1/3 cup sesame seeds
3/4 cup whole raw almonds
3/4 cup sliced almonds
3/4 cup honey
1 teaspoon pure vanilla extract
1 1/2 cups golden raisins

Toast the oats (see page 13), then combine with sunflower seeds, sesame seeds, and almonds in a large bowl. In a saucepan, combine the honey and vanilla, and warm until the honey melts and becomes "liquefied." Add the mixture to the dry ingredients and stir thoroughly to combine and coat completely with honey.

Spread in a thin, even layer in roasting pans or jelly-roll pans. Bake, stirring and respreading often, until light golden brown. Pour granola into a large bowl and quickly stir in the raisins.

For a clumpy granola, while still warm, press into a 1-inch layer with even edges. Allow to cool; then remove in sections and store in an airtight container. To serve, crumble to desired chunkiness.

Tropical Granola

6 cups rolled oats
3/4 cup sunflower seeds
1 cup unsweetened shredded coconut
2 cups nuts, any of the following alone or in combination:
  macadamia, pistachios, cashews, brazil nuts, hazelnuts
1/2 cup honey
1/3 cup canola oil
1 1/2 cups dried banana chips and/or chopped dried pineapple,
  papaya, pears, apricots

Preheat oven to 325°F.

In a large bowl combine the oats, sunflower seeds, coconut, and nuts. In a saucepan warm the honey and oil until hot, but not boiling. Then add to the oats mixture and stir until thoroughly combined and well-coated. Spread in thin, even layers in roasting pans. Bake, stirring and respreading frequently, until light golden brown — 15-20 minutes. Turn granola into a large bowl and stir in the dried fruit.

Gingerbread Granola

4 cups rolled oats
1 cup whole wheat pastry flour
1 teaspoon cinnamon
1 teaspoon ginger
1/4 teaspoon cloves
1/4 teaspoon nutmeg
1/2 teaspoon cardamom
pinch of salt
1 cup pecans
1/4 cup unsalted butter, melted, or canola oil
1/2 cup honey
1/4 cup molasses
1/2 chopped dried apricots or dates (optional)

Reminiscent of the classic cookie . . .

The addition of butter, flour, and molasses gives this granola a chewy, crumbly texture.

Preheat oven to 325°F.

In a saucepan, add the honey, molasses, and spices to the melted butter or canola oil. Gently warm, stirring to blend spices and release their flavors. In a large bowl, combine the oats, flour, and pecans. Pour in the honey mixture and mix thoroughly. Spread in thin, even layers in a roasting pan. Bake, stirring often, until golden, about 20 minutes. If desired, stir in dried fruit directly after granola is removed from oven.

Maple Walnut Orange Granola
(with poppy seeds)

Popular and easy to come by . . .

"English" or "Persian" walnuts (easily identified by their tan skin) are mild in flavor and best complement the subtle flavors in this recipe.

6 cups rolled oats
$^1/_2$ cups walnuts
4 tablespoons poppy seeds
$^2/_3$ cup maple syrup
$^1/_2$ cup honey
$^1/_4$ cup canola oil
zest of 1 orange, minced
1 $^1/_2$ cups raisins

Preheat oven to 325°F.

Toast the oats (see page 13), then add to a large bowl with the walnuts and poppy seeds. In a saucepan, blend together the maple syrup, honey, oil, and orange zest; heat until hot, but not boiling.

Add to the oats mixture and combine thoroughly. Bake in thin even layers in roasting pans or jelly-roll pans, stirring frequently, until golden brown — about 20 minutes. Pour granola into a large bowl. Stir in raisins while the granola is still warm. Then let cool completely before storing in an airtight container.

Apple Walnut Granola

6 cups rolled oats
1 1/2 cups walnuts (see note on previous page)
1/4 cup molasses
1/2 cup maple syrup
1/2 cup honey
1/4 cup canola oil
1 1/2 cups chopped dried apples

Note:

If desired, replace some of the dried apples with chopped dates and/or figs.

Preheat oven to 325°F.

Combine the oats and the walnuts in a large bowl. In a saucepan, gently warm together the molasses, maple syrup, honey, and canola. Add to the oats and mix thoroughly. Spread in thin, even layers in roasting pans. Bake, stirring every 5 minutes, until golden and crisp. Remove from oven and stir in dried apples. Pour into a large bowl and allow to cool before storing in an airtight container.

Apricot Cashew Granola

6 cups rolled oats
1/4 cup sesame seeds
1/2 cup sunflower seeds
1 cup raw cashew halves
1/4 cup molasses
3/4 cup honey
1 1/2 cups chopped dried apricots

Preheat oven to 325°F.

Toast the oats (see page 13). Combine with the sesame seeds, sunflower seeds, and cashews in a large bowl. In a saucepan, gently warm the molasses and honey. Add to the oats mixture and mix until all is thoroughly combined and coated with the honey. Spread in thin, even layers in roasting pans. Bake, stirring and respreading every 5 minutes, until crisp and golden brown — about 20 minutes. Remove from oven and stir in the chopped apricots. Press into an even layer and allow to cool in a solid mass. Break at random to desired clumpiness.

Very Granola
(makes 8 cups)

2 cups rolled oats
2 cups rolled barley
1/2 cup raw wheat germ
1/2 cup sunflower seeds
1/4 cup sesame seeds
1/2 cup almonds
1/4 cup flax seeds
1/2 cup walnuts
1/2 cup honey or maple syrup (or 1/4 cup of each)
1/4 cup molasses
1 cup raisins
1/2 cup chopped dried apricots
1/2 cup shredded, unsweetened coconut

Note:

Use any combination of rolled grains to equal 4 cups.

Preheat oven to 325°F.

Toast the rolled oats and barley (see page 13), then combine with sunflower seeds, sesame seeds, flax seeds, almonds, and walnuts. In a saucepan, heat the honey (and/or maple syrup) with the molasses until hot (do not boil). Add to the grains mixture and mix thoroughly. Spread in thin, even layers in roasting pans. Bake, stirring on occasion, until golden, 15-20 minutes. Remove from oven and stir in raisins, apricots, and coconut. For clumpy granola, press still-warm granola into a 1-inch thick layer and allow to cool completely. Break at random into desired clumpiness.

COMPLETELY NUTS
Granola as an Ingredient...

BREADS

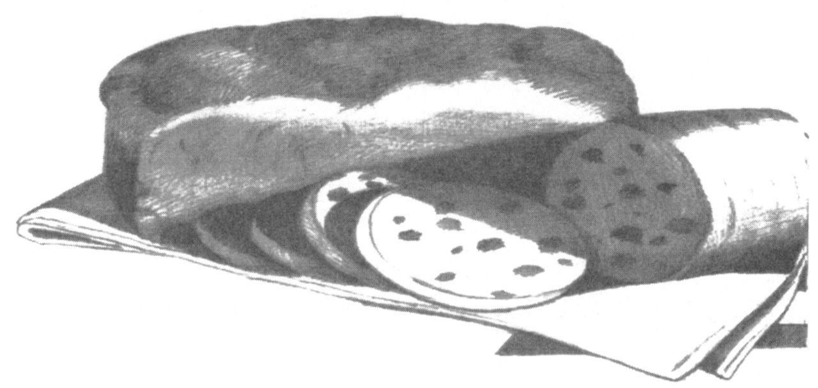

Whole Grain Granola Bread

Scald milk by . . .

heating to 198°F, not quite to boiling, for 1 minute, or 185°F for 7 minutes, before using in doughs. This treatment appropriately alters the milk proteins to effectively react with the flour's (wheat's) proteins to build a stronger dough. Don't forget to let it cool before combining with yeast.

1/2 cup honey
3 1/2 cup lowfat milk, scalded
3 tablespoons active dry yeast
1/2 cup rolled oats
3/4 cup stone ground cornmeal
1 cup rye flour
2 cups Honey Almond Granola
1 1/2 cups whole wheat flour
1 tablespoon salt
2 eggs
1/2 cup canola oil
4 cups (more or less) all-purpose flour

Preheat oven to 375°F.

In a small saucepan: scald the milk. Remove from heat and add the honey. Cool to lukewarm, then stir in yeast until dissolved. (Scalding then cooling the milk is a necessary step. It alters the milk proteins so that their interaction with the flour's protein is compatible in order to give the dough its needed strength.) Cover and let proof until bubbly — 10 minutes.

In a large bowl (ideally a heavy-duty mixer), combine oats,

cornmeal, rye and wheat flours, granola, and salt. Add eggs and oil to yeast mixture, then add to dry ingredients, mixing until well combined (with a dough hook, if using the mixer).

Begin adding the all-purpose flour one cup at a time, mixing to incorporate each addition, to make a sticky dough. Continue to knead for five minutes with dough hook, or remove to a floured surface to knead, adding dustings of flour as needed to keep dough from sticking.

Let the dough rise in a large oil-coated bowl covered with plastic wrap or a damp heavy towel until doubled — 1 hour.

Dump dough onto a well-floured surface and shape into two loaves: press each piece of dough into a 9-inch x 15-inch rectangle.

Then fold like a letter, pinching together the seam and ends. Place, seam side down, in oiled 5-inch x 9-inch bread pans. Cover the loaves with a tea towel and let rise until doubled — 40-60 minutes. Bake for 20 minutes at 375°F, then turn oven down to 350°F to finish baking — another 15-20 minutes.

Proofing:

Once dry yeast is rehydrated in warm (105° - 110°F) water (or milk) it can reach its ideal condition for its activity. We are allowing it to "proof" or prove that it's active.

Dark Granola Soda Bread

To "sour" a cup of milk . . .

use room temperature milk (70°F). Place 1 tablespoon of lemon juice or distilled white vinegar in a measuring cup; then fill with milk to equal one cup. Stir and let the mixture stand for 10 minutes. It will have the consistency of cultured buttermilk or yogurt.

3 1/2 cups whole wheat flour
3/4 cup all-purpose flour
1 cup Orange Pecan Granola
2 tablespoons unsweetened cocoa
2 tablespoons packed brown sugar
1 tablespoon baking soda
1 1/2 teaspoons salt
about 3 cups buttermilk or sour milk

Preheat oven to 375°F.

In a large mixing bowl combine flours, cocoa, sugar, baking soda, and salt. Mix thoroughly to distribute baking soda; stir in granola. Add enough buttermilk to make a soft, biscuit-like dough. Knead lightly for 2-3 minutes. Shape into a round loaf. Place on a greased or parchment-lined cookie sheet. Slash a cross on top of the loaf with a sharp knife dipped in flour. Bake until loaf is browned and sounds hollow when tapped on the bottom — 35-45 minutes. Cool, then slice thinly.

Granola Brown Bread

(a quick yeast bread, with no kneading, and only one rising)

2 cups whole wheat flour

$^1/_4$ cup all-purpose flour

1 cup granola (with sunflower seeds, walnuts, and/or dried apples)

5 teaspoons active dry yeast (1 $^1/_2$ packages)

2 cups warm water (105°-110°F)

2 tablespoons molasses

1 tablespoon salt

Parchment paper . . .

assures that cakes, breads, etc., will release perfectly from baking pans.

Preheat the oven to 450°F.

Butter a 5-inch x 9-inch x 3-inch loaf pan. Place the flours and granola in a mixing bowl and set in a warm oven (150°F) for 10-15 minutes, stirring once or twice to evenly warm the flour and granola. In the meantime: in a glass measuring cup, dissolve the yeast in $^1/_2$ cup of warm water; then stir in the molasses. Let the yeast proof; then add another $^1/_2$ cup of water.

Add the salt and the yeast mixture to the warmed bowl with the granola and flour. Stir in enough water to make a sticky dough (about 1 cup or more depending on how much the flour absorbs). Put the dough directly into the prepared pan, cover with a damp cloth, and let rise to one-third its size. Bake until the crust is nicely browned and the loaf sounds hollow when tapped.

Remove from the pan and leave the loaf in the turned-off oven for about 15 minutes to take on a crisper crust.

Granola Fruit and Nut Bread

1 package (1 scant tablespoon) active dry yeast
2 tablespoons honey
1/2 cup warm water (100°-105° F)
1/4 cup (1/2 stick) unsalted butter, cut into pieces
1 3/4 cup milk
5-6 cups all-purpose flour
2 teaspoons salt
1 cup granola (including dried fruits and/or nuts)

If a fruitless and nutless granola is what you have on hand...

use dried fruits and/or nuts to supplement — any combination of almonds, walnuts, or hazelnuts, and dried apricots, figs, dates (chopped), or raisins.

A total of 1 cup combined granola and dried fruits and/or nuts is needed.

In a large bowl combine the honey and warm water; stir in the yeast and allow to proof for 10 minutes. In a saucepan, scald the milk; remove it from the heat, add the butter and salt, then allow to cool to lukewarm; add to the yeast mixture. Stir in the flour, one cup at a time, beating well after each addition. When the dough becomes too stiff to stir, remove to a well-floured surface and begin kneading, adding small amounts of additional flour as needed to make a soft, smooth, springy dough.

Shape the dough into a ball, coat with a bit of softened butter, place in a lightly buttered bowl. Cover with a heavy damp towel and allow to rise in a warm place until doubled in bulk.

Preheat the oven to 400°F.

Punch the dough down, turn out onto a floured surface, cover (invert the bowl over it), and let rest for 5 minutes. Sprinkle the granola over the surface of the dough, then knead thoroughly and evenly to incorporate. Cut the dough in half and shape into two loaves by pressing the dough into a flat rectangle. Then, pinching the seam with your thumbs with each turn, roll into a sausage shape, about 9 inches long. Place in two buttered 5-inch x 9-inch x 3-inch bread pans. Cover loosely with a dry tea towel and allow to rise until the dough comes to the top edges of the pans. Bake for 30 minutes. Remove the loaves from the pans and return to the oven shelf to bake for about 10 minutes longer. The loaves are done when the crusts are golden brown and the loaves sound hollow when tapped on the bottom. Allow to cool on rack before slicing.

Granola Molasses Bread
(quick bread)

1 1/2 cups Queen Granola or Apple Walnut Granola
1 cup whole wheat flour
1 cup all-purpose flour
1 teaspoon salt
1 teaspoon baking soda
1 teaspoon baking powder
1 large egg, lightly beaten
1/3 cup unsulfured molasses
1 1/4 cup buttermilk

TOPPING:
1 tablespoon cold unsalted butter
2 tablespoons dark brown sugar
2 tablespoons flour
1 teaspoon cinnamon
1/4 cup Raw Granola, coarsely chopped

In a bowl combine granola, the flours, salt, baking soda, and powder. In a larger bowl, whisk together the sugar, egg, molasses, and buttermilk. Add the granola mixture and stir the batter until just combined. Divide batter into 2 greased (3 1/2-inch x 7 1/4-inch x 2 1/4-inch) loaf pans.

Make the topping: blend the brown sugar, butter, flour, cinnamon, and granola until the mixture is crumbly, and sprinkle the topping over the batter. Bake in the middle of the oven until a skewer inserted in the center comes out clean — 45-50 minutes. Let the loaves cool in the pans, on a rack, for 10 minutes. Remove loaves from the pans and cool for 2 hours before wrapping to store in refrigerator (up to 1 week) or freezer, or serve warm with jam or some softened cream cheese.

Spiced Apple Granola Bread
(quick bread)

1 1/2 cups Honey Almond Granola
1 cup all-purpose flour
1/2 cup whole wheat flour
1 teaspoon salt
1/2 teaspoon baking soda
1 teaspoon baking powder
2 teaspoons cinnamon
1/4 teaspoon ground ginger
1/4 teaspoon fresh grated nutmeg
3 tablespoons unsalted butter, softened
1/3 cup firmly packed brown sugar
2 large eggs, lightly beaten
1 cup buttermilk
1 Braeburn, McIntosh, or Fuji apple, peeled, cored, and chopped

Preaheat the oven to 350°F.

In a bowl, combine thoroughly the flours, granola, salt, baking soda and powder, cinnamon, ginger, and nutmeg. In a larger bowl, combine butter, sugar, and eggs. Whisk in the buttermilk. Add the dry ingredients and the chopped apple, and stir until just combined. Divide the batter between 2 greased 3 1/2-inch x 7 1/4-inch x 2 1/4-inch loaf pans and bake in the middle of the oven until a skewer inserted in the center comes out clean. Let the bread cool in the pans on a rack for 10 minutes, then loosen and turn the loaves right side up onto the rack to cool completely (to store), or serve warm with apple butter or toasted with butter and cinnamon sugar. The bread keeps, wrapped tightly and chilled, for up to 5 days or it may be frozen.

Apricot Bread

$3/4$ cup boiling water
1 cup dried apricots
$1/2$ teaspoon baking soda
$2/3$ cup sugar
2 eggs
2 $1/2$ cups all-purpose flour
3 teaspoons baking powder
1 cup Honey Almond Granola

Preheat the oven to 350°F.

Pour the water over the apricots and let them soak until they are tender (just tender; don't let them get mushy). Drain the water from the apricots into a glass measuring cup; add more water if needed to measure 1 cup. Chop the apricots.

In a medium bowl, combine the flour, baking powder, granola, and apricots. Pour the liquid into a larger bowl, and whisk in the baking soda, sugar, and eggs; add the granola mixture and stir until thoroughly combined. Divide the batter between 2 greased and floured 5-inch x 9-inch x 3-inch loaf tins. Bake until the loaves are dark in color and a skewer inserted in the center comes out clean — about 45 minutes. Cool on rack in pans for 10 minutes; serve warm.

Sweet Yeasted Curry Pumpkin Bread

$^1/_2$ cup warm water
3 tablespoons active dry yeast
4 tablespoons unsalted butter
2 $^1/_2$ tablespoons curry powder
$^3/_4$ cup honey
1 cup buttermilk
1 cup pureed pumpkin, butternut, or acorn squash (see page 16)
1 tablespoon salt
1 $^1/_2$ cups Gingerbread, Tropic, or Apricot Cashew Granola
6-7 cups all-purpose flour

Stir the yeast into the warm water until dissolved and creamy; set aside and let proof for 15 minutes. Melt butter in a saucepan over medium-low heat; add the curry powder and cook for 1 minute (to release flavor and cook out chalkiness). Remove from heat and stir in honey, buttermilk, and puree, add the yeast mixture; combine well. Stir in 3 cups of flour to make a smooth batter-like mixture. Cover with a heavy damp towel; set aside for about 30 minutes — this sponge will become bubbly and rise slightly.

Stir in the granola, 2 cups of flour, and the salt. Continue adding flour, one cup at a time, until the dough is too stiff to stir. Turn out onto a floured surface and knead, adding additional flour to make a smooth, soft dough. Shape the dough into a smooth ball. Place in a generously buttered large bowl, turning it over a few times to coat with butter. Cover with the heavy, damp towel and let rise until doubled in bulk — about 1 hour.

Preheat the oven to 425°F.

Punch down the dough. Divide into 2 pieces. Shape the loaves to fit into two 4-inch x 8-inch x 2½-inch bread pans. Place in buttered pans and allow to rise until doubled in size. Brush the tops with melted butter and make one ½-inch-deep slash with a sharp knife along the length of the loaves. Bake until browned — about 35 minutes. Remove the loaves from the pans; return them to the oven to finish browning the lower crusts for about 12-15 minutes. Test for doneness by tapping bottoms, listening for hollow sound.

Cool on rack before slicing.

Lemon Bread with Honey Almond Granola

4 ounces unsalted butter

1/3 cup sugar zest of one lemon, finely chopped

3 eggs

1/2 cup fresh lemon or orange juice

2 cups all-purpose flour

1 cup Honey Almond Granola (loose crumble, almonds chopped)

3 teaspoons baking powder

1 teaspoon salt

Preheat oven to 350°F.

Butter and flour a 4 1/2-inch x 8-inch x 2 1/2-inch loaf pan. Sift together the flour, baking powder, and salt; stir in the granola. In a large mixing bowl, cream the butter and sugar until fluffy; add the lemon rind and the eggs, one at a time, beating well after each addition. Stir in the lemon juice. Add the dry ingredients gradually, mixing well with each addition until you have a light but sturdy batter. Pour the batter into the prepared pan and bake for 50-60 minutes. Turn out onto rack; cool completely before slicing.

Granola Bread Pudding

1 loaf Whole Grain Granola Bread (crust removed, diced)

3 cups milk

4 eggs

1/2 cup sugar

1 1/2 teaspoons vanilla

1/4 teaspoon nutmeg (ideally fresh ground)

2 tablespoons softened unsalted butter

TOPPING

Combine the following:

1/2 cup brown sugar

2 teaspoons cinnamon

1 teaspoon nutmeg

Preheat oven to 375°F.

Spread the cubed bread on a baking sheet and allow to dry out for 4 hours or overnight. In a large bowl beat the eggs and sugar together until lemon-colored and thickened. Slowly whisk in the milk; then add the vanilla and the spices and blend well. Add the dried bread to the egg mixture and let stand, stirring occasionally, for 45 minutes.

Butter a 2-quart baking dish and coat with half of the topping. Spoon the bread pudding into the dish and cover with a buttered piece of foil. Bake the pudding in a water bath (in the oven, by placing the pudding in a roasting pan with 1 to 1 ½-inch of water) for 1 hour. Remove the foil, dot the top with butter and sprinkle with the remaining topping. Bake, uncovered, for another 15 minutes.

Granola Bread Stuffing

½ cup (1 stick) unsalted butter
1 loaf (1 lb.) Whole Grain Granola Bread cut into ¾-inch cubes
2 cups diced onion
2 cups finely diced celery
2 cups chopped apples (Braeburn)
½ cup chopped dried apricots (dried cranberries or cherries)
1 tablespoon fresh sage, chopped (1 ½ teaspoon, dried)
1 teaspoon fresh rosemary, minced (½ teaspoon, dried)
1 cup chicken or vegetable stock
salt and pepper to taste

Note:

Use cake flour or whole wheat pastry flour for a more delicate pancake.

Spread the bread cubes in single layers on baking sheets. Toast until lightly browned in a 325°F oven. Set aside in a large mixing bowl. Heat ¼ cup of the butter in a large skillet over medium heat and sauté the onions and celery until soft and translucent — 3-5 minutes. Add the apples and dried fruit; sauté briefly, then season with the herbs, salt, and pepper and cook for 2 more minutes. Add to the bread cubes.

Heat the chicken stock. Add the remaining ¼ cup butter. When the butter is melted, pour over the bread mixture while tossing. Use to stuff poultry or game birds, or bake at 250°F in a buttered 9-inch x 13-inch baking dish, covered with foil until heated through — about 25 minutes.

Granola Pancakes

2 1/2 cups granola (with sunflower seeds, sliced almonds, and/or raisins)
1 cup whole wheat flour or 1 1/4 cups all-purpose flour
1 tablespoon baking powder
1 teaspoon salt
2 tablespoons brown sugar
1 tablespoon canola oil
1 egg
2 cups milk

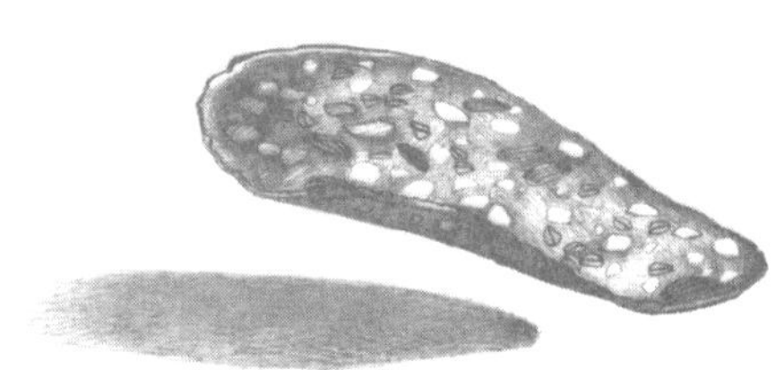

Thoroughly stir together the granola, flour, baking powder, and salt. Whisk together the oil, egg, and milk. Add the dry ingredients to wet and stir just to combine. Cook on a hot greased griddle until browned on both sides.

Granola Bread French Toast

3 large eggs
1 cup milk
2 tablespoons sugar
1 teaspoon pure vanilla extract
1/4 teaspoon cinnamon
1/8 teaspoon baking powder
8 slices of Whole Grain Granola Bread, 1-inch thick
2 tablespoons unsalted butter

Note:

Reduce fat in this recipe by using low-fat milk. To use half the butter in the recipe, cook in a nonstick skillet.

Whisk together the first 6 ingredients to combine thoroughly. Place bread in a large shallow baking dish and pour egg mixture over the top; turn each piece of bread to coat evenly. Press a piece of buttered wax paper directly onto the bread to cover. Refrigerate overnight. To cook, start with one tablespoon of butter in a large skillet. When butter begins to foam, add the bread to the pan (do not crowd) and cook until brown on both sides. Cook the bread in batches, adding more butter as needed.

COOKIES

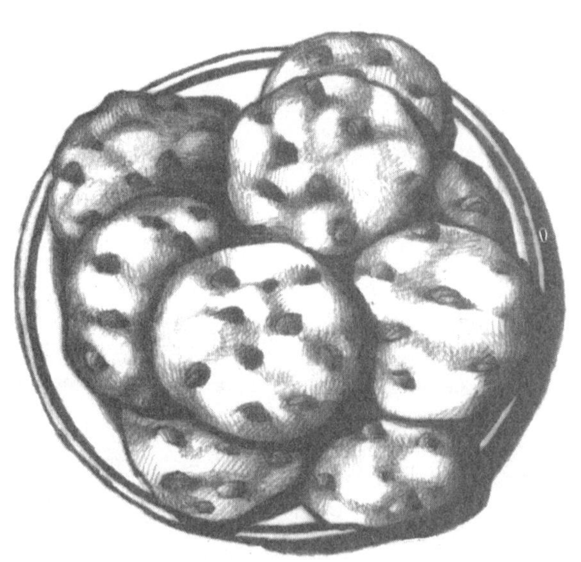

Granola Date Bars

2 cups pitted dates
grated rind of 1 orange
½ cup orange juice
6 ounces (1 ½ sticks) unsalted butter, cut into cubes, softened
1 cup all-purpose flour
½ teaspoon salt
¼ cup firmly packed light brown sugar
¼ cup granulated sugar
2 ½ cups Simple Granola

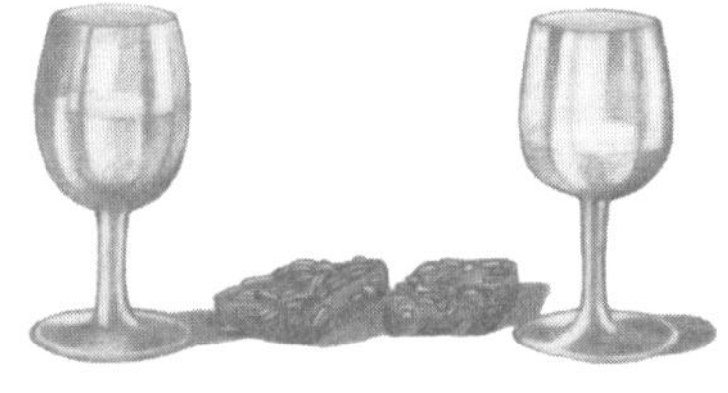

Preheat oven to 375°F.

In a saucepan combine the dates, the rind, the orange juice, and ½ cup water. Bring the mixture to a boil; then reduce to a simmer, mashing the dates with a fork and stirring; cook for 3-4 minutes. Remove the pan from the heat and let the puree cool.

In a bowl combine butter, flour, salt, sugars, granola, and blend well with your fingers. Press half the granola mixture evenly into the bottom of a greased 9-inch x 13-inch baking pan. Spread the date mixture over it in an even layer, then finish with the remaining granola mixture. Bake in the middle of the oven for 30-40 minutes, or until golden. Let cool completely in the pan, and then cut into bars.

TWICE BAKED GRANOLA BARS

1 cup all-purpose flour
1 teaspoon cinnamon
1 teaspoon baking powder
1/4 teaspoon salt
1 1/2 cups granola with almonds
6 tablespoons unsalted butter
1/2 cup sugar
1 egg
2 egg yolks
1/2 teaspoon vanilla extract
Candied Orange Zest (optional) (see page 105)

Preheat oven to 350°F.

Butter and flour a baking sheet, or line with parchment paper. Combine thoroughly the flour, cinnamon, baking powder, salt, and granola. In a mixing bowl, cream the butter with the sugar, beating until light and fluffy. Beat in the egg, one of the yolks, and the vanilla. Sprinkle the dry ingredients over the creamed mixture and gently fold together. Chill the dough for 30 minutes to an hour.

On a lightly floured surface, roll the dough into a 10-inch x

12-inch rectangle. Roll the dough up onto the rolling pin and unroll onto the prepared baking sheet. Repair any tears with your fingers. Beat the remaining egg yolk and brush over the dough. Bake until shiny and pale golden — 12-15 minutes. Remove from the oven and reduce the temperature to 325°F. Cut the rectangle diagonally into 1 ½-inch wide strips; cut the strips into 2-inch lengths. Return the bars to the oven to toast until golden — about 10 minutes.

Chewy Granola Squares

$^{1}/_{2}$ cup unsalted butter
$^{3}/_{4}$ cup firmly packed light brown sugar
1 tablespoon light corn syrup
$^{3}/_{4}$ teaspoon salt
1 teaspoon vanilla
2 cups Simple Granola

In a saucepan melt the butter over low-medium heat, stir in the sugar, the corn syrup, the salt, and the vanilla; bring to a boil, stirring occasionally. Remove from the heat and stir in the granola. Spread the mixture evenly into a buttered 9-inch x 13-inch baking pan; bake in the middle of preheated 350°F oven for 20 minutes. While still warm, cut into squares and let cool in the pan on a rack. The squares will harden as they cool.

Very Granola Bars

Note:

For a less-sweet granola bar, replace the honey with brown rice syrup.

3 cups raisins
1/2 cup water
1/2 cup honey
1/2 cup whole wheat pastry flour
2 teaspoons vanilla
4 1/2 cups Very Granola
1/2 cup applesauce or apple butter

Bring water to a boil; add raisins and simmer, stirring for 2 minutes. Drain, then add to all other ingredients and mix well. Bake in an oiled 9-inch x 13-inch pan at 350°F for 20 minutes. Cool; then cut into bars.

Granola Shortbread

1/2 cup unsalted butter
3/4 cup plus 2 tablespoons all-purpose flour
1/2 teaspoon salt
3/4 teaspoon cinnamon
2/3 cup Maple Pecan, Maple Walnut Orange,
Apricot Cashew, or Honey Almond Granola
1/3 cup firmly packed light brown sugar

Preheat oven to 300°F.

Combine the flour, salt, and cinnamon. Cream the butter; adding the brown sugar, beat until the mixture is light and fluffy. Add the flour mixture to the butter mixture and the granola, and stir until just combined. Press into a 9-inch pie pan, smoothing the top, and pricking all over with a fork. Bake in the middle of the oven for 40 minutes, until golden. While the shortbread is still warm, score it with the tines of a fork all the way through into wedges. Let it cool completely in the pan on a rack. Break into wedges.

Giant Chocolate Chip Granola Cookies

1 ½ sticks (6 ounces) unsalted butter, softened
⅔ cup firmly packed light brown sugar
⅔ cup granulated sugar
1 teaspoon pure vanilla extract
2 large eggs
1 ¾ cups all-purpose flour
¾ teaspoon baking soda
¾ teaspoon salt
1 cup semi-sweet chocolate chips, or coursely chopped bittersweet or white chocolate
1 cup Maple Pecan Granola

Preheat oven to 350°F.

Sift together the flour, baking soda, and salt. In a large bowl with an electric mixer, cream the butter. While beating, add the sugars and beat the mixture until it's light and fluffy. Add the vanilla, beating until it is well incorporated; then add eggs, one at a time, beating well between each addition. Add the flour mixture and beat until well combined. Stir in the chocolate and granola. Drop ¼-cup measures of the batter 3 inches apart onto lightly greased or parchment-lined cookie sheets. Press lightly with wet fingers into ½-inch thick rounds. Bake in the middle of the oven until light golden brown — about 15 minutes. Remove to a rack or brown paper bags to cool. Makes about fifteen 5-inch cookies (or two dozen 2-inch cookies).

Citrus Granola Cookies

2 cups all-purpose flour
1 $1/4$ cups sugar
2 teaspoons baking powder
1 teaspoon baking soda
1 teaspoon salt
1 teaspoon nutmeg
1 teaspoon cinnamon
2 sticks (1 cup) unsalted butter, softened
2 eggs
1 tablespoon fresh orange juice
1 tablespoon lemon juice
3 teaspoons minced orange zest
2 teaspoons minced lemon zest
2 $1/2$ cups granola (with raisins, almonds, pecans, and/or honey)
$1/2$ cup semi-sweet chocolate chips (optional)

Preheat oven to 375°F.

Sift together the flour, baking powder, baking soda, salt, nutmeg, and cinnamon. In a large bowl with an electric beater, cream the butter and sugar; add the eggs, one at a time, beating well between each addition. Add the lemon and orange juice, beating until smooth. Stir in the lemon and orange zest, the granola, and optional chocolate chips. Drop tablespoons of the dough onto lightly greased or parchment-lined cookie sheets. Bake until light golden brown — about 15 minutes. (Makes 5-6 dozen.)

Hazelnut Almond Granola Biscotti

3 cups all-purpose flour
1/2 cup ground toasted almonds
2 teaspoons baking powder
1 teaspoon cinnamon
1 cup Apricot Cashew Granola (use hazelnuts instead of cashews)
5 eggs
4 ounces (1/2 cup) unsalted butter, melted
1 1/2 cups sugar
1 1/2 teaspoons chopped lemon zest

Preheat oven to 350°F.

Sift together first four ingredients then stir in the granola. Whisk the eggs until frothy; stir in the butter and lemon zest. Add the dry ingredients to the egg mixture and stir until just combined and the mixture comes together into a sticky dough. Divide the dough into 4 pieces and, with lightly floured hands, shape each piece into a 2-inch x 12-inch log, placing them 3 inches apart on a lightly oiled or parchment-lined cookie sheet. Bake in the middle of the oven, turning pan once, until lightly golden and beginning to crack on top — 30-40 minutes. Cool the loaves for 10 minutes. Lower the oven to 325°F.

With a serrated knife, cut the loaves diagonally, into ½-inch slices. Lay the slices ½ inch apart on the cookie sheet and return to the oven to toast 10 minutes on each side until crisp and golden.

Cool completely to assure that all moisture has escaped before storing in an airtight container.

MUFFINS, SCONES, BUSCUITS, ETC.

Granola Muffins
(an even dozen)

2 cups all-purpose flour
1/2 cup sugar
2 teaspoons baking powder
1/2 teaspoon baking soda
1 cup Maple Pecan Granola
1/4 cup canola oil
1 cup plain, non-fat yogurt
2 eggs
1 teaspoon vanilla extract

Preheat oven to 350°F.

Sift together flour, sugar, baking powder, and baking soda. Stir in the granola. In a larger bowl, whisk together the oil, yogurt, eggs, and vanilla. Add the dry ingredients to the yogurt mixture and stir gently until just combined. Line a muffin tin with paper liners (or grease the muffin tin cups generously). Spoon the batter into the cups until nearly full and bake until a skewer inserted into the center comes out clean — about 20-30 minutes. Serve warm.

Pumpkin Ginger Granola Muffins
(12 muffins)

1 cup cake flour
1 cup Gingerbread Granola
1/2 teaspoon baking powder
1/2 teaspoon baking soda
1/2 teaspoon salt
1/2 cup packed light or dark brown sugar
1/4 cup buttermilk
2 eggs
3/4 cup pureed pumpkin, acorn or butternut squash, or sweet potato (see page 16)

Preheat oven to 350°F.

Sift together baking powder, baking soda, flour, and salt. Stir in granola. Beat together the eggs and sugar, stir in the buttermilk and the puree; add the granola mixture, and stir gently until just combined. Line a muffin tin with paper liners or grease and dust evenly with flour. Spoon the batter into the cups until nearly full. Bake until a skewer inserted into the center comes out clean — about 20 minutes.

Spiced Carrot Banana Granola Muffins
(14 muffins, a dozen plus 2 for the cook)

Allspice . . .

is a small reddish brown berry with a mixture of cinnamon, clove, nutmeg, and juniper berry flavors.

1 1/2 cups whole wheat flour
2 teaspoons cinnamon
1/2 teaspoon baking soda
1 teaspoon baking powder
1/2 teaspoon ground allspice
1/4 teaspoon cloves
2 cups Gingerbread Granola or Simple Granola with dried apricots and almonds added
1 1/2 cups shredded carrots
2/3 cup plain yogurt
1/2 cup mashed banana (or applesauce)
1/2 cup fresh orange juice
1/4 cup honey
1 tablespoon grated orange zest

Preheat oven to 350°F.

Grease and flour muffin cups or line with muffin paper liners. Sift together first 6 ingredients, then stir in granola. In a large bowl, thoroughly combine the remaining ingredients; then add the dry ingredients and gently fold until just combined. Fill muffin cups to nearly full. Bake until golden brown and a toothpick inserted into the centers comes out clean — about 20 minutes. Cool briefly in tins; then remove to rack.

Orange Marmalade Chocolate Chip Muffins

1 cup whole wheat flour
1/2 teaspoon baking powder
1/2 teaspoon baking soda
1/4 teaspoon salt
1 cup Honey Almond Granola
3 eggs
1/4 cup thick-cut orange marmalade
1/4 cup mild-flavored honey or (packed) light brown sugar
1/2 cup milk
1/2 cup bittersweet chocolate chips

Preheat oven to 350°F.

Grease and flour muffin cups or line with paper muffin liners. Sift together flour, baking powder and soda, and salt. Stir in the granola and chocolate chips. In a large bowl whisk together eggs, marmalade, honey, and milk. Add the dry ingredients and stir just until flour is moistened. Spoon into prepared muffin cups, filling to nearly full. Bake until a skewer inserted in the centers comes out clean — 20-25 minutes.

Apple Walnut Zucchini Muffins

1 cup all-purpose flour
$^1/_2$ teaspoon baking powder
$^1/_2$ teaspoon baking soda
1 teaspoon cinnamon
$^1/_2$ teaspoon ginger
$^1/_4$ teaspoon ground cloves
$^1/_4$ teaspoon salt
1 cup Apple Walnut Granola
2 large eggs (or 3 large egg whites)
$^1/_3$ cup sugar
$^1/_4$ cup safflower or canola oil
2 cups grated zucchini, firmly packed

Preheat oven to 350°F.

Grease and flour muffin cups or line with paper muffin liners. Stir together, combining thoroughly, the first 8 ingredients. In a large bowl, whisk together the eggs, sugar and oil; stir in the grated zucchini; add the dry ingredients and stir until just combined. Spoon the batter into the muffin cups filling until nearly full. Bake until a skewer inserted in the center comes out clean — about 20 minutes.

Banana Muffins with Maple Pecan Granola and Cocoa

1 cup whole wheat flour
1/3 cup sugar
1 teaspoon baking powder
1/2 teaspoon salt
6 tablespoons cocoa
1 cup Maple Pecan Granola
1/2 cup raisins (if they are not in the granola)
2 large eggs
2 tablespoons safflower or canola oil
3 extra-ripe medium bananas (1 1/2 cups), mashed

Preheat oven to 350°F.

Grease and flour muffin cups or line with paper muffin liners. Stir together, combining thoroughly, the first 6 ingredients. Add the raisins. Whisk together the eggs and the oil, then combine with the mashed bananas. Stir the dry ingredients into the banana mixture until just combined. Spoon the batter into the muffin cups filling until nearly full. Bake until tops are cracked and golden brown — 20-25 minutes.

Hearty Whole Grain Granola Muffins

2 1/4 cups Very Granola
2 1/4 cups buttermilk
1/2 cup packed light or dark brown sugar
2 eggs
1/4 cup canola oil
1 cup whole wheat flour
1 cup all-purpose flour (or cake flour)
1 3/4 teaspoons baking soda
1 1/2 teaspoons baking powder
1 teaspoon salt

In a large bowl, whisk together the buttermilk, eggs, sugar, and oil. In a smaller bowl, combine the flours, baking soda, baking powder, and salt; stir in the granola. Add the dry ingredients to the liquid ingredients and stir until just combined. Spoon the batter into muffin cups, filling each almost full. Bake until the edges are brown and tops spring back when touched — about 15 minutes.

Lowfat Muffins

A granola with no oil, no seeds, and no nuts will make this muffin virtually fat-free, though a fistful of sliced almonds would be a nice addition. The following recipe makes a dozen standard-size muffins.

1 cup cake flour
1 cup Raw Granola or Writers' Granola (no oil recipes)
2 teaspoons baking powder
1/2 teaspoon baking soda
1/2 teaspoon salt
2 egg whites
2 tablespoons molasses
1/4 cup nonfat evaporated milk
3/4 cup unsweetened applesauce

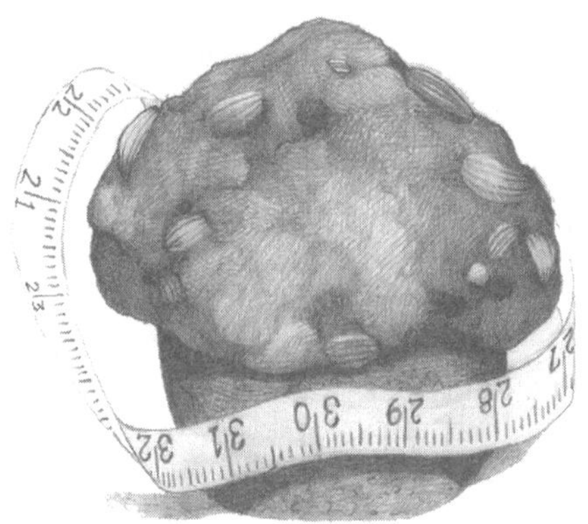

Preheat oven to 350°F.

Grease and flour 12 muffin cups or line with paper muffin liners. Combine the flour, granola, baking powder, baking soda, and salt. In a large bowl whisk together the egg whites, molasses, milk, and applesauce. Add the dry ingredients to the wet and stir until just combined. Fill muffin cups three-quarters full; bake until a toothpick inserted in the center comes out clean — about 20 minutes.

Ginger Pumpkin Scones

1 cup all-purpose flour
2 teaspoons baking powder
1 teaspoon salt
1 teaspoon cinnamon
1/4 teaspoon ground cloves
1 teaspoon ground ginger
4 tablespoons unsalted butter, chilled, cut into small pieces
1 cup Writers' Granola
2/3 cup pumpkin or sweet potato puree (see page 16)
2 egg yolks, plus 1 whole egg
2 tablespoons honey
1/2 cup milk
1 teaspoon sugar

Preheat oven to 425°F.

Sift together the flour, baking powder, salt, and spices. With your fingers, rub the butter into the dry ingredients until the mixture resembles coarse meal. Stir in the granola. Whisk together puree, egg yolks, honey, and milk; add to the granola mixture and stir only until moistened.

Turn the dough onto a lightly floured surface and toss it

lightly (and briefly) until smooth on the outside. Pat or roll into a ¾-inch thick round. Cut into 6 wedges. Brush with the beaten whole egg and sprinkle with the sugar. Bake until shiny and golden brown — about 15-20 minutes.

Note:

Omit the ground ginger and add 1½ tablespoons candied ginger for a sweeter, more intense ginger flavor (see page 106). Add the candied ginger to the recipe with the granola.

Scones with Candied and Golden Raisins

1 ½ tablespoons Candied Orange Zest, finely diced (see page 105)
1 ½ tablespoons golden raisins
1 tablespoon brandy, Madeira, or bourbon (optional)
1 cup all-purpose flour
½ cup Honey Almond Granola
1 ½ teaspoons baking powder
½ teaspoon salt
1 ½ tablespoons, plus 1 teaspoon sugar
4 tablespoons unsalted butter, cut into small pieces
2 eggs
⅓ cup milk

Preheat the oven to 425°F.

Place the orange zest and golden raisins in a small bowl and toss with the brandy, or with warm water. Allow to soak and plump for 15 minutes. In a large bowl combine thoroughly the flour, baking powder, salt, and 1 ½ tablespoons sugar. Rub the butter into the mixture until it resembles coarse meal. Stir in the granola.

Stir the orange zest and raisins into the dry ingredients (drain them if they have not absorbed all their soaking liquid). Beat together the eggs and the milk. Reserve 1 tablespoon of this mixture, and add the remaining to the dry ingredients. Stir until just moistened, when mixture begins to form a dough. Turn dough onto a lightly floured surface and knead gently for a few seconds. Pat into 3/4-inch thick round and cut into 6 wedges. Brush the tops with the reserved egg mixture and sprinkle with the remaining 1 teaspoon of sugar. Bake scones on a greased or parchment-lined cookie sheet until golden brown — about 15 minutes.

Granola Biscuits

1 1/2 cups flour
1/2 cup Simple Granola
1 tablespoon baking powder
3/4 teaspoon salt
6 tablespoons unsalted butter, cut into bits
3/4 cup milk

Preheat oven to 400°F.

Combine dry ingredients and rub in butter. Stir in milk with a few strokes to form a soft dough and turn it out onto a floured surface. Knead the dough lightly for a few seconds; pat into a disc 1 inch thick. Place on a greased or parchment-lined baking sheet. Score the dough into 8 wedge portions (leaving the disc intact) and bake until browned — 12-15 minutes.

Sweet Potato Granola Biscuits

1 cup all-purpose flour
4 teaspoons baking powder
1 teaspoon salt
1/2 cup Maple Pecan or Apricot Cashew Granola
4 tablespoons unsalted butter, chilled, cut into small pieces
3/4 cup mashed sweet potato
2/3 cup milk

Note:

Canned pumpkin or fresh puree of pumpkin, acorn or butternut squash can replace the sweet potato (see page 16).

Preheat the oven to 450°F.

Sift the flour, baking powder, and salt together. Rub the butter into the mixture until it resembles coarse meal. Stir in the granola. Whisk together the milk and sweet potato then add it to the dry ingredients. Stir until just moistened, when the mixture begins to form a dough. Turn the dough onto a lightly floured surface and toss it lightly (and briefly) until it is smooth on the outside. Pat it into a 3/4-inch thick round. Cut into 6 wedges. Bake on lightly greased or parchment lined cookie sheet until golden brown — about 15 minutes.

Granola Coffee Ring

DOUGH

1 package (1 scant tablespoon) dry active yeast

1/2 cup sugar

1/4 cup warm water (100°-105°F)

1 cup milk, scalded

1/4 cup (1/2 stick) unsalted butter

2 egg yolks, plus one whole egg, lightly beaten

2 teaspoons salt

3 1/2 - 4 1/2 cups all-purpose flour

FILLING

1/4 cup melted unsalted butter

1 cup Maple Walnut Orange Granola (leave out poppy seeds; add raisins, chopped figs, or dates)

3 tablespoons brown sugar

For the dough, combine the yeast with the warm water and 1 tablespoon of sugar; allow to proof for 10 minutes (see page 15). Stir the softened butter, the salt and ½ cup of sugar into the scalded milk and allow to cool to lukewarm; add to the yeast mixture. Add the flour, one cup at a time, beating after each addition to make a loose dough. Turn the dough onto a floured surface and begin kneading, adding additional flour as needed to make a soft, smooth dough that is only slightly springy when touched. About 5 minutes of kneading is enough; overkneading will toughen the dough and hinder the rising. Coat the dough with softened butter and place it in a lightly buttered bowl. Cover with a heavy dampened towel and let rise until doubled in bulk — about 1 1/2 hours.

Preheat oven to 375°F.

Punch the dough down and turn it out onto a floured surface. Let it rest for a few minutes; then gently roll and stretch the dough into a 12-inch x 18-inch rectangle. Brush the surface with the melted butter and sprinkle evenly with the brown sugar and granola. Roll a rolling pin over the filling to embed it into the dough. Starting from the long edge, roll up the dough like a jelly roll, pressing each seam with your thumbs as you go. Pinch the ends together to form a ring. Place the ring on a buttered or parchment-lined baking sheet. Make slashes two-thirds of the way deep into the ring at 1-inch intervals. Twist each section to the right so that the interior of each is facing upward. Cover lightly with a dry tea towel and let rise in a warm place until doubled in size. Brush with beaten whole egg. Bake until browned — 30-35 minutes. Cool on a rack for 10 minutes before serving.

STICKY BUNS

These luxurious treats can be made from the Coffee Ring recipe. The brown sugar, pecan topping, and the honey glaze add a few more steps to the process, but it is time well spent. Use the same recipe for the dough. Maple Pecan Granola filling would add the classic touch, but there is room to experiment.

FILLING

1/2 cup packed dark brown sugar

1 cup Maple Pecan Granola (or one that stirs your imagination)

1 1/2 teaspoons cinnamon

1/4 teaspoon nutmeg

1/4 teaspoon cloves (If the spices are already in the granola, you may want to use less spice, or none at all. Make adjustments to suit your taste.)

2 tablespoons unsalted butter, melted

BROWN SUGAR GLAZE

6 ounces unsalted butter, melted

1 cup packed light brown sugar

HONEY SYRUP

3/4 cup honey

4 ounces unsalted butter

Prepare the pans with the brown sugar glaze: grease the sides of two 10-inch round cake pans (not springform). Pour half the melted butter into each, and sprinkle each with half the brown sugar; set aside.

Place all the filling ingredients, except the melted butter, in a bowl. With your fingers, crumble the granola into a fine, uniform consistency, and combine everything thoroughly.

Preheat oven to 375°F and set oven rack to middle position. After you have rolled the dough into a 12-inch x 18-inch rectangle, brush the surface with the melted butter and sprinkle the filling evenly leaving a ½-inch border along the long edges. Roll a rolling pin over the filling to embed it into the dough. Starting from a long edge, roll up the dough into a tight log. Loop a piece of dental floss or nylon thread around the log, cross the ends and pull them to slice into 1 ½-inch pieces. Place the buns, cut side down, into prepared pans. Cover with a damp towel, and let rise 50 percent. Bake until buns are golden brown — 25-35 minutes.

Make the syrup: combine honey and butter in a saucepan. Simmer for 2-3 minutes to thicken slightly. As buns come out of the oven, pour the syrup over them. Shake the pans a bit to distribute syrup and loosen the buns. Use a thin spatula to separate the buns from the edge of the pans. To remove buns, immediately invert the pans onto rimmed baking sheets (to catch any extra syrup).

Cool for 10 minutes before serving.

Note:

Toast a handful of pecans, chop them roughly, and sprinkle over the buns after they come out of the pans. Add more raisins, or some chopped apricots to the filling if the granola used for the filling lacks dry fruit.

COBBLERS, DESSERTS, AND TOPPINGS

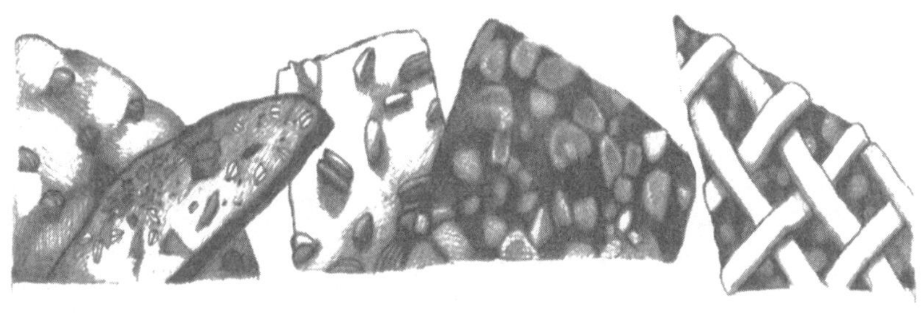

Fresh Fruit and Granola Cobbler

8-10 cups of berries, peeled and sliced fresh peaches or nectarines, fresh pitted cherries, or a combination of these
1/2 cup sugar
juice of 1 lemon
1/2 cup (1 stick) unsalted butter
1/3 cup sugar
1 egg, lightly beaten
1 cup flour
2 teaspoons baking soda
1 cup Simple Granola or Honey Almond Granola
1 cup buttermilk

Preheat oven to 350°F.

Combine the fruit with the sugar and the lemon juice. Set aside. Stir together the flour, baking soda, and granola, combining well. Cream the butter adding the sugar until light and fluffy; beat in the egg. Stir the dry ingredients into the butter mixture alternately with the buttermilk. Spread the batter in a buttered and floured baking dish. Cover with the fruit. Bake 45-50 minutes, or until fruit is bubbly, juices are caramelized, and the cake is firm (test with the point of a knife or a skewer).

Morning Fruit Crumble

A wonderful warm way to enjoy fruit and granola. A little plain yogurt completes your breakfast — great for dessert too. Seasonal fruit variations makes this recipe right for any time of the year. In the late spring and summer, when berries, peaches, apricots, and nectarines are in season, choose those fruits.

2 ripe, juicy peaches or nectarines, or 4 fresh apricots (Rub the fuzz off the peaches and apricots as best you can with a damp towel, without bruising the fruit, or, if inclined, slip the skins off after blanching them in boiling water for 30 seconds.)
1 cup blueberries (or blackberries, marionberries, raspberries)
2 teaspoons fresh lemon juice
1 cup Raw Granola
1/3 cup all-purpose flour or whole wheat pastry flour
1/3 cup packed brown sugar
3 tablespoons cold, unsalted butter, cut into pieces

Preheat the oven to 400°F.

Lightly butter a 9-inch pie plate or casserole dish. Split the peaches and discard the stones; cut the halves into cubes. Toss with the berries and lemon juice. Pour into prepared baking dish.

Combine the granola, flour, and brown sugar; work the

butter in with a pastry cutter or your fingers. Sprinkle the crumble over the fruit. Bake until the fruit is bubbly and the tops are browned — 20-25 minutes.

Other fruit combinations:

bananas and blueberries with fresh grated ginger, cinnamon, and a pinch of cloves.

Upside Down Pear Tart

1 tablespoon unsalted butter
$^{1}/_{3}$ cup packed light brown sugar
2 large, firm, ripe pears (Bosc or Anjou), peeled, cored, cut into $^{1}/_{4}$-inch slices
1 cup all-purpose flour
$^{1}/_{2}$ cup Honey Almond, Apple Walnut, or Maple Pecan Granola
2 teaspoons baking powder
2 teaspoons baking soda
1 teaspoon salt
2 tablespoons cold unsalted butter, cut into pieces
$^{2}/_{3}$ cup buttermilk

Preheat oven to 425°F and place rack in lower third of oven.

In a 7-inch or 8-inch oven-proof skillet, heat 1 tablespoon butter over medium heat. Add the brown sugar and cook, stirring, until sugar is half melted — 1 or 2 minutes. Remove from heat and arrange pear slices in an overlapping circular pattern, pressing them into the sugar. Set aside. In a bowl, combine flour, baking powder, soda, salt, and granola. Work the cold butter into the mixture with a pastry cutter, or quickly, with your fingertips, until the mixture resembles course meal. Add the buttermilk and stir until just combined. Drop spoonfuls of the dough evenly over the pears. Place the skillet on a baking sheet and bake until a toothpick inserted in the center comes out clean — about 20 minutes. Let cool on a rack for 2 or 3 minutes. Carefully loosen the tart from the skillet by running a stiff spatula around the edge and invert the tart onto a plate. Serve warm with ice cream or frozen yogurt.

Baked Bananas, Mangoes, and Peaches with Fresh Ginger and Coconut Macadamia Nut Granola

Start with perfectly ripe peaches and mangoes so that the flow of the fruit's natural juices mingles with the honey to make a fresh fruit and syrup sauce. The contrasting warm/cool, smooth/crunchy textures can be further enlivened with the tang of fresh ginger and "exotic" additions to the granola.

1 mango, peeled and sliced,
1 large peach, sliced
2 firm ripe bananas, sliced
juice from half a lemon
2 tablespoons honey
1 teaspoon grated ginger (optional)
$^1/_2$ - $^3/_4$ cup Tropical Granola
fresh or frozen berries (optional)

Preheat the oven to 350°F.

In a large wide bowl, gently toss the fruit with the honey, lemon juice, and optional ginger. Arrange the fruit in an even layer in baking dish. Cover with foil. Bake for 15 minutes. Remove foil and finish baking for another 10 minutes, until fruits

How to choose a perfectly ripe mango:

Choose firm, unblemished mangoes that are on the large side. The skin may be green or yellow, turning red and yellow as the fruit ripens. A ripe fruit will yield to gentle pressure and will smell sweet and delicious. Mangoes will ripen at room temperature fastest in a perforated paper bag. Store ripe mangoes in a plastic bag in the refrigerator; they will last a few days.

are glazed and beginning to brown on top. Sprinkle the granola over the fruit and keep warm in the just-turned-off oven while you finish making a stack of pancakes or waffles. Or serve immediately with ice cream, yogurt, or pound cake.

Note:

If using frozen berries, add them still frozen.

Candied Citrus Zest

Remove the zest (rind) from oranges, lemons, grapefruits, or limes with a vegetable peeler. Using long even strokes, working from top to bottom, cut away wide strips leaving behind the pith (all the pith — clean away any that remains on the strips). Cut the zest into thin julienne strips.

For each cup of citrus zest: In a saucepan, cover with ¾ cup cold water. Bring to a boil over low heat. Simmer for 10 minutes, drain. Repeat this process; then drain well. In a saucepan, combine ¼ cup water and ½ cup sugar. Bring to a boil. Add the zest and simmer until syrup is absorbed and the peel is transparent. Watch carefully to keep from burning, shaking the pan to stir occasionally. Dredge each piece of zest in sugar and allow to dry thoroughly on rack. Store in airtight container in the freezer.

Candied Ginger

¼ cup peeled fresh ginger root, cut into ¾-inch strips
½ cup water
⅓ cup sugar

Blanche the ginger: in a saucepan, with water to cover, bring to a boil, then drain. Add the ½ cup water and sugar. Over low heat, simmer until ginger is tender and the syrup is clear, shiny, and reduced slightly — about 20 minutes — shaking pan occasionally to keep from scorching. Keep warm if you are using it right away, or store in a tightly covered container at room temperature. The ginger will keep indefinitely.

Dried Fruit Compote

Any combination of dried fruits works for this recipe — vary them as you will.

4-5 cups of unsweetened dried fruits: currants, cherries, apples, pears, dates, figs, apricots, and/or peaches
zest of 1 orange, finely slivered
1/4 cup sugar
2 tablespoons honey
1 tablespoon fresh lemon juice
1 stick cinnamon
1 cup dry red or white wine
1 cup water

Cut the large dried fruit pieces into strips; leave the small ones whole.

Combine all in a nonreactive saucepan. Bring to a boil; then reduce heat and simmer for 20 minutes. Remove the cinnamon stick. Remove the fruit with a slotted spoon, and continue to cook the liquid until it reduces to a light syrup. Pour the syrup over the fruit. Cool before serving with Granola Shortbread or Lemon Bread with Honey Almond Granola.

Fresh Fruit Preserves

These preserves are simple — the essence of ripe summer fruits with a minimum of sugar — and will keep well refrigerated and freeze beautifully. Serve as a sauce or spread on muffins or biscuits.

Peach, Nectarine, or Apricot Preserves
(one quart)

4-5 cups (about 3 lbs.) sliced, peeled, fresh peaches, nectarines, or apricots
2 1/2 cups sugar
2 tablespoons fresh lemon juice

Reserve all the juice when peeling and slicing the fruit. Then gently mix with the fruit slices, the lemon juice, and sugar in a stainless steel, glass, or ceramic mixing bowl. Let it sit for 4-5 hours.

Place the mixture in a heavy nonreactive saucepan and cook, simmering over low heat until the liquid is clear and the fruit is translucent — 20-25 minutes. Remove the fruit with a slotted spoon, and continue cooking the syrup until it reduces by half — another 20 minutes — stirring occasionally. Add the fruit back to the syrup, return to a simmer. Pack into sterile jars or freeze in airtight plastic containers.

Berry Preserves
(one quart)

Blueberries, raspberries, blackberries, or gooseberries can be used to make these preserves.

4 cups fresh berries
2 cups sugar
3 tablespoons fresh lemon juice

Following the recipe for the Peach, Nectarine, or Apricot Preserves, macerate the berries for 45 minutes; cook for 5 minutes before removing the fruit and reducing the syrup.

About the Authors

Donna Wallstin has degrees in Creative Writing from Stephens College in Columbia, Missouri, and Culinary Arts from New England Culinary Institute. She has worked as a professional cook in a variety of positions, from a five-star restaurant in Napa Valley, to cooking on Whidbey Island, Washington, as a chef for Cottages at Hedgebrook, a writers' retreat. She is currently writing and teaching in Seattle.

Katherine Dieter has been writing and editing for more than fifteen years. She has contributed to several books, most recently *Spirit Moves* by Loree Boyd, published by New World Library. This is the story of six generations of Native American women. She currently lives in Mill Valley, California.

If you enjoyed *Granola Madness*, you might be interested in other cookbooks published by New World Library, including:

Vegetarian Food for All
The Vegetarian Lunchbasket
and
Cooking for Consciousness

New World Library is dedicated to publishing books and audiocassettes that improve the quality of our lives. Our books and tapes are available in bookstores everywhere.

For a catalog of our complete library of fine books and cassettes, contact:

New World Library
14 Pamaron Way
Novato, CA 94949

Phone: 415-884-2100
Fax: 415-884-2199

Or call toll-free: 800-227-3900